Letters to Forget

Letters to Forget

POEMS

Kelly Caldwell

ALFRED A. KNOPF

NEW YORK

2024

THIS IS A BORZOI BOOK PUBLISHED BY
ALFRED A. KNOPF

www.aaknopf.com

LIBRARY OF CONGRESS CATALOGING-IN-PUBLICATION DATA
Names: Caldwell, Kelly, 1988–2020, author.
Title: Letters to forget : poems / Kelly Caldwell.
Description: First edition. | New York : Alfred A. Knopf, 2024. | "This is a Borzoi book"—title page verso.
Identifiers: LCCN 2023054431 (print) | LCCN 2023054432 (ebook) | ISBN 9780593538012 (hardcover) | ISBN 9780593538029 (ebook)
Subjects: LCGFT: Poetry.
Classification: LCC PS3603.A4366 L48 2024 (print) | LCC PS3603.A4366 (ebook) | DDC 811/.6—dc23/eng/20231211
LC record available at https://lccn.loc.gov/2023054431
LC ebook record available at https://lccn.loc.gov/2023054432

Jacket art by Kelly Caldwell
Jacket design by Chip Kidd

Manufactured in the United States of America
First Edition

1st Printing

CONTENTS

✦✦
✦

Self-Portrait as Job

✦✦
✦

Unlearning the Letter

NOTE TO THE READER

Kelly died on March 23, 2020, at the age of thirty-one, after living with the diagnosis of bipolar 1 disorder for nearly four years. At the time of her death, she had two manuscripts of poems. This one, the first manuscript, was finished. Only the most minor editing went into preparing these poems for publication. To have Kelly's voice in the world, to have her poems reach readers, would mean everything to her.

—CASS DONISH

Promise Light or Tomorrow

[house of apocalypse]

I am the last woman.
In the world.
Lie on the deck without breasts.
In the world. Behind.
A bird to peck eyes out.
I have had a thousand children.
All with tin edges.
A hook to lead them.
A spool to unwind eternity.
Rest is only bridge stanchions.
I own a great dread.
I have had a thousand children.
Tie them to.
The trunk.
For vacation.

[dear c.

The night is so quiet

you wouldn't even notice it on your electric bill. 3:00 a.m. seems an ordinary time to be awake. I don't even pray. I traveled through the day to get here, in a car with you, lover, and a friend. I brought books—these ones to read and these others to wear around my body. The nurse pokes her head around the door to check for breathing. She is a winnower, sifting through our groans and fears, which pour out like grain, like spilt drink. Three silent girls sit at a common table. One of them wishes for death unforthcoming. My knees stiffen. It's not a drama, just stones sewn into pockets. My mouth pressed against glass. Flat miles and two white deer that wait for the conflagration. If this glass is edible, I will not go hungry.

[house of rope]

No one promised light or tomorrow.
Time slipped down or over.
The glass jaw line. Cropped out.
Sing I am Blessed I am blessed.
But what a strange party with
Fewer players than melodies.
Jangling harsh the making of future.
Furrows. Turns out that the taste of red.
Is like pennies or a poorly cast.
Bell. To assist the hoist.
This place has a stained rug and.
Blind-slats. Just a length of rope, baby.

[dear c.

Oconomowoc, Wisconsin,

just before rainfall. As if the moon illuminated anything but walls, this sad septic world. I have needed your help, even now. *Amor fati* tattooed on a therapist's twitching foot: surely something will come of this, some innocence or splendor, some healing or blistered heel. *I am new, I am new, I am new*. My language, though, is spoiled: it doesn't know I am made new. Some poet once claimed that the sun was slag, burning, losing bits of itself off the sides. The Greeks, after killing him, lay god-blind in the shade of a ledge's hip. One day, a final burning coin, an eaten magnitude, will be minted and spin down, clarifying and consuming the sawed-off shotgun clouds, the wind coming cold off the lake, this little paradise, its final shine.

[house of now]

At first she refuses to sing.
Because the philosophers said.
There is no now to be had.
Independent of the thing having
The now. Her voice is like a gecko.
At the window or like a tin bucket.
Under rain. It arrives drowning.
The bare geometry of hand.
Moving from here to there.
She thinks that time only matters.
Because her soul is between her teeth.
And either you or I are wrong.

[dear c.

I wish I spoke

like a French philosopher. I wish my words rested thick and querying in my open-shut-open mouth. I wish my intellect was in mourning for metaphysics. I wish I had the nerve to lounge shirtless in cut-offs on a summer couch with the window open and French philosophy in my mouth and you on my lap. I wish you and I fucked like adults. Or talked like adults. I wish you would write a book where I appeared as a central character. I wish you wouldn't mention my hand tremors, which shake me up like a head rising from sand. I wish starlings carpeted the floor of this rainy April morning instead of a beige spread. I wish I knew if this were living or just a dense accumulation of moments, forming a dumb convoy, like geese under midwestern skies.

[house of Kafka]

Kafka said guilt is never to be doubted.
That man feels guilty
Is alone enough to establish.
In atonement he surrenders.
His keys his idleness his hairline.
His magician's box.
His hands curled in desire.
The faint smell of cigarette smoke.
On his jacket. Guilt opens its bag.

[dear c.

I am ashamed.

I haven't kept my body parts properly greased. They go spinning on a tent rope burn. My mind scuttles its own doctrine of reason and dances on the mast. High on propane, fogged and singing a song of spillage. Named and unnamed we mud magpies contemplate flight but to no end, the air yellowed in a late disposition. Hold my wrist until the scar arrives. Memory is an occult terrain and desire drives the Ezekiel wheel it rides on. To judge the distance properly requires a postscript, a letter after the original file is erased. Here are some awkward questions, and you can say what you're thinking. How many bruises can I put on the scale before it tilts? How much does a marriage bed weigh? How to place this actual body on an actual body? If given the chance, should I cut up a man like a tiled fish? What I mean is, this nerve-strung bridge, does it lead always in one direction? My elbow slips its hinge. That is not what I meant at.

[house of brick]

We made an offer on the house now what.
Now the substance and the property.
Now the backyard with a louche
Clothesline and a latched metal gate.
Dandelion down on interior layers.
Of salt and shout. Windows wait.
For some sound to blow them out.
Of their frames and welcome a fresh.
Rain. Loneliness sits beside the swing.
Kicks its feet idly. An occupied house.
Can be absolutely solitary.
Today a wedding anniversary.
Undoing and undone the clothesline.
Swings under weak fingers. The whole.
Of the house waits inside the circle.
Of thumb and forefinger. Debt.
Is its own reward.

[dear c.

John Berryman had his Henry

to dance his brittle bones like an old tree scourged white in the wind. The enormous tragedy of his dream bent his shoulders like a Mexican bullock. Consist, he said. Or perhaps, persist. Sadness removed the verdict of his mouth like a jury, like a cat walking in a metallic cloud across the moon. Hundreds, oh hundreds. Fleas and the drag of a dog. John, we should lay hold of the earth, we should walk free like Barabbas. We should become familiar, learn each other's knuckles, coin-slot spines, tuck-clam cocks. When we jump from our bridge toward the water on the river's west bank. We will be the bitter skin of a grape. The gap between the teeth of a child. The tremble of a telephone. *Hello?* answers the lover.

[house of sorrow]

The sun shines always it seems.
I am the child of a last farmer.
They partitioned the land.
For a long highway. A waste of what.
Split birch and piano dust.
Sorrow is a settler of flesh.
Me and sorrow, we've exhausted.
Each other. The dead would give anything.
Sorrow won't take them back.

[dear c.

From a young age, the child

dreamed of being other than it was. It would soak itself in the bath to encourage greater plasticity in its flesh. It felt itself made of small things. Then smaller. It arranged round river stones in front of it and tapped on them, as if to wake the birds inside, to make their lancet beaks scrape against the hard scalps of the stones. When the sun was hot enough that moving in and out of the shade felt like moving a hand in and out of water, it took off everything but a dingy white hat and rubber boots with the toes cut out and walked in a circle, repeating the word "clothes" to itself until the word curled up its legs and fell apart. It wrote itself a letter: "I am living here with a stranger."

[house of roses]

Domesticity waits in my mother's hands.
Like shadows wait on the sun. She says.
Write down your symptoms of melancholy.
On a sheet of paper a map.
Unfit for the virtuous.
She swims in the round lake detached.
From memory. Wisdom is a defense.
Morality is a fence. To climb over.
Match to edge of paper.
Doll. I cannot get this dress on.
She crayons in the flame.
Hands the garment my moth beats.
Like film frames the darkness between.
My colorless body a static image of
A cassette flame blossoming like breasts.

[dear c.

I find my griefs

and music in other people's journals I buy in thrift stores. I feed off girls who hold out lyric sweetmeats in their curried palms. I strut like a blue heron. Description is a bulwark—but here's how it is now, an escarpment. I have no excuse to be inside, since day has come, and the pink apples are harvested and cut. Please, don't mind me, I'm standing facing the wall, trying to pay off a debt. The sloping night will bring the collector. The collector will come with the likeness of a man, with the face of a man, and wings, and the hands of a man holding a full syringe. My tapping brain orates double time against the bland plaster. I'll bring dancing to the streets of Argos, having slipped the tight-chested place where most of us live. I copied down paragraphs of love letters culled from those old journals and sent them to my mother with no return address. Mother shameful and strobe-blinded. Dear mother, the floor is tilted, the birds are falling faster, and the rats are moving in. For real this time.

[house of family]

That was a movie seen just once.
We sing hymns. Bitch dog rolled.
Under the van. Dear lord children walk.
With synchronized steps
And a rivet of grief.
They have taken our parents.
Away. Downstairs at the stove.
Clatter two strangers.

[dear c.

Once, on its grandfather's farm,

the child found the remains of a small vineyard. Green, rasp-teethed grape leaves with high frames to encourage their growth. Behind was a small summer shed no longer in use. Nothing on the farm was any longer in use. The cows no longer moved across the field pulled with the sun. Milk cows no longer the better clocks, the grandfather never having bothered to set his own clock to anything else. The child didn't know that the red-bulbed grapes hanging in clusters were wine grapes. It hadn't yet tasted wine. When it put a grape in its mouth, the skin of it was thick and bitter and the flesh sweet and full of seed shot. It spat it out and dropped the rest from its hands, ground them into the grass with the rubber heel of its shoe. It started stripping the vines from the trellis, strewing them about. It took off its clothes and its shoes and jumped up and down on the grapes until the red pulp stained its feet and the vines bit at its white instep and their acid smell opened up in the sun's chiaroscuro. It pulled up the grape clusters that were left and broke them open on its chest and down over its bony hips. And after, the child in the summer shed, wiping down its legs and feet with its underwear, which it left behind when it went, stained, sticky, its skin sugared and itching, to the slanting, peeling gray house with its slate roofs.

[house of secret]

Delilah ruffles Samson's.
Hair in preparation for blade. Before he tells her.
His secret she ruffles his hair.
He tells her about nightmare.
"Stone fell and crushed me."
Is a woman someone.
Without strength.
Or someone with long hair.
Samson asleep she.
Takes out cigarette puts it back she.
Parts curtain of hair.
The shorn hair. Braids.
It into her own and goes.
Out into the unflexed muscle of night.

[dear c.

Where there are no dreams

night rainy. In dream in the recesses of throat and chest. The inhale and exhale is like the thrum of wheels echoing in tunnel. Sometimes sobbing. Sometimes nocturnal groans like from the body of Christ. Just a small catalogue of terror. While in bed, around ten in the evening, peacefully reading—it would be dishonest if I told you I remembered which book—the walls of my hospital room began to disappear. Frightened, I looked around. No walls remained at all, as far as I could see, but that wasn't very far, despite having nothing obscuring my line of sight. A loudspeaker bellowed from somewhere above my head, the voice curt but disinterested: "in accordance with the decree on this day, the twenty-second, on the abolition of memory and its replacement with electricity." The bed disappeared also, and my body seemed without nature. My hands, soft and curled as ferns, pawed at my chest, which had stopped moving with my breathing but had instead grown a great swinging udder. I seemed to be repeating the words "If necessary, I will give up my eyelids." Where there are no dreams. I once tracked a doe from our garden to where it had slept in a stand of pines. A bed of needles.

[house of body]

Poor them. Their body unknown.
Like a foreign.
Currency. Untradeable for any.
Crust of bread. Stick figure hopes.
For grave marble uninscribed. Suck.
On a hungry man's chest. Suck.
Two breasts and a head on a platter. Parts.
Don't add up without history.
Nouns wish a new nearness like
Water absorbing into a towel.
Eyelashes of milk and water drag.
On their cheek. A low-slung sky.
With no forehead. Tread on this ground.
Like on a floe of ice.
Step forward. Step forward.

[dear c.

I confess to loneliness.

It is absent any stage, fieldstripped of lies. It sings itself an anthem, come closer now to hear it. Furious and empty sings the gut. I rhapsodize, but it's like a couple of inverted letters on a typewritten page. The key caps switched. Did I say loneliness sings? It is as mute as the curve of my thumbnail. But what goes on when you talk about loneliness? It doesn't dissipate, it merely shifts places in your body. Right now it's lodged like salt in my kidneys. Look for a cure, warm evenings and a fuck a sudden mouth a warm thread of red as good as any wire snare. I enter myself as an explorer and the stark jumble of my dismemberment knots me up, pretty boy. Dream vision where have you been? I give my clavicle as an oar to the waiting boatman. The river is extinct but the boatman still smells of fish, scales rank and silver. He says blankface that he can get me home. His drop torch to the shale crumbles brought to heel at the river bed. At the river's mouth is a door unbolted and open.

[dear c.

Talk to a madman

who claims he is a demon who claims he is a fish who claims he is the cave water over the place where the eyes of a blindfish should be who claims you are a woman. Undress in front of him to show him your body without fins and without breasts. Undress a madman. Undress the truth by talking to a madman. Take a madman seriously. Find that it is impossible to disagree with a madman. It is not so much his joy in the geometry of tables as his insistence that there is no place to put the chairs. Seize the madman and hold him and ask him which he prefers, to change or to tell the future. Talk to a madman who tells you to find, under the livid ribs of a carcass, a swarm of bees. Decide if it is meat or honey that you need.

Let me be a pretty flute girl on your arm. You'll think I'm a torch.

[dear c.

Sometimes, after I wake up,

I think that I smell like an animal. Not a lot, perhaps not even noticeably. But the sheet sticks to me too closely, and there is a thin sweat around my waist. I feel like I am hemorrhaging fear. Come under my arms and taste the air for me. I think I smell like an animal.

[dear c.

Last night you told me

about a dream you once had, in which you experienced omniscience. You dreamed yourself in a library, holding a book you knew better than memory; you dreamed yourself watching a VCR and running the tape backward on every man; you dreamed yourself a symphony of all the sound in the world, the whistle of day to day rushing past, and you dug your heels in and took the sound into yourself like into a well, only to give it back. Imagine the bodies, dismembered and clarified. This is what the living do. You made them out of your hair. You filled their mouths with drops of milk from your breast. I believe you were a benevolent consciousness netting all the accretions in the world, all the pearls built up better than love. The flesh a blue swarm. Our knowledge of this, the grateful silt of forgetfulness. Your hand kept opening toward eternity.

[house of left hand]

Seize the inclination.
Toward a lathed new life. Turn.
The hard knurl of pink nipple.
Never yet held but it seems
You might have offset the bite.
Like the squeak of ice between.
Glass-crowned teeth. We cast.
Time wanton and without.
Survivor. Colors supplied.
By our minds' nerve towns. Lie down.
Who wouldn't embrace the right.
Hand's absence and in its place.
What it is that the moment.
Wanted and couldn't find.

[dear c.

You’re writing something to me

that you couldn’t say out loud. You’re writing smoldering things, the page has turned in on itself, it has curled back and covered your fingers with little smears of ash. Finger tapping articulates time, not eloquently as in running grains of sands within a poised and symmetrical glass, but plainly enough. Don’t send me whatever it is in the letter. Show me the inside of your lip where you’ve tattooed an aleph. Show me, instead, your hair underwater.

[house of bare life]

An event emerging out of a rigid logic.
A woman sits in a meadow.
She removes a blade of grass.
The meadow is still a meadow.
She removes another blade of grass.
The meadow is still a meadow.
She removes all the grass.
Glues the grass to her fuzzy dress.
The meadow is still there.
Only now it is also a naked plot of dirt.

[dear c.

Will you kindly care for my garden

until I return? It is spring now, early, and I've planted it in neat rows, pushing lithium into the loam with my thumb. My watering has prepared for the ferning of the plants, the gloss of the leaf, hose made of heart bivalve blue rubber stretched out, running water out of temporal lobes where the chromatic function sits. It's delicately cracked, like a window after a bird flies into it. I planted the garden for my health. The proper posture of the world, sucking water on all fours. Can I ask again later if you would do me the kindness? Watch the salt growths, the noisy masses of nerve song. The air will smell of salt and the dirt will turn to sand. The house is not far from the garden—you can take shelter during heavy rains, orphan imprints awash. I will return, turning in psalmody. A moon might appear. I will return.

[house of house]

I lied that it was fun.
That I would do it again.
I looked back the house.
I looked back. The house.

A billion
Years. Turn over like.
A restaurant table. I think.
I am the only guest.

When do I graduate
From the symbolic.

I am not old but winter leans.
To wind.
After all that time to fall.
Asleep. The house is the same.
Except for my bad dreams.
In which I dream that it is.
Spring.

Self-Portrait as Job

✦✦
✦

SELF-PORTRAIT AS JOB

Here are the credences of summer

/

Here is the land fertile and wide The movement of growth toward
 flesh in the juniper root
The centuries an ascending sum and reclining
Small gaps Open wide their mouths as for rain
Gentle flesh carrying in the great sleep a storm Headless There is
 no mapping this
The monstrous cloud our love
Attachments bare and thin like gruel are given away in error
Body vaguely wrong like a piece from a different board

Also the distance of the fields

Also the proximity of the sunlight

/

There was a man
Whose name was Job
Whose life accumulated lateness
Who couldn't uncouple
His good fortune
From his guilt
In the morning Lay your head
On the altar cool and with Bladed
Eelgrass
Burn your hair

In an offering
To
god

/

His children all before him in neat sets, seven sons and three daughters and four corners
Of
The house inside of which they lived
Job, considered,
Lived in a different house with a wife who wore her long hair up on her head and
Moved
With a great burden of hair weighing her down until her face
Began
To run like quicksilver
How
Stiff her walk from the sink to the table looking out across the salt
Flats
Protecting the home
Inside
The house another house Inside Job's red ribs wherein the
Pumping
Heart lived, another heart was strung

/

Satan came wandering east The accuser The stranger in the field
Who yields the harvest He knew
About burnt He knew

The ash smoke left after a burn He
Had had the filthy altar pointed out from heaven He
Looked at the torn cattle carcass and the smoke spires
A little bored really To be honest
They say there is a war but
This has been going on for a long time
And no real reason to stop
god and him more alike than they ever admitted Both
Wore faces to the dice table They had picked
Job because he was always counting up his livestock
And was, you know, impossibly without sin

Put forth your hand now and touch his bone, only spare

/

Job's wife at the kitchen table Her actions all internal
Job was out back, later later, laying with a camel boy
Who was lean and brown and whippet-like
All my darlings, he said, Or maybe Oh my darling
And maybe he was talking to the camel boy or maybe
His wife who wiped the table in Endless circles until
The sealant came off in tiny fingernail peels that smelled
Of citrus Oh my said Job to the camel boy Hear me out:
What you think is a hot plate coil heating red in your mouth
Is the taste of shame Spit or swallow it
Either way it may take quiet root

/

Perfect and upright
Job is without a shadow He
Gets nervous Like the long jump of the sun's mark

Has been cut without cicatrice
He keeps a constant eye on the weather
When he is in the house he looks outside
To see if he can spot any small singed
Shadow, but he is sinless

/

god put forth his long hand like a timing chain
Which drives a toothed wheel
Like a long knowledge of what acts are now before us He
Didn't bother with celestial light
And touched Job, exhumed his debt
Which had been there all along Wide
And wide awake his Wife prepared to exit
Decomposed
For as shadows of ourselves We
Appear false in the false grass
Which is only green until it is not

/

It is summer, so there is no rain. The house
It is summer, so there is no memory. The house
It is house, so there is no sound. The rain
It is field, so there is no flood. The memory
It is half, so there is no whole. The house
It is gone, so there is no image. The gift
It is a child, so there is no sparrow. The child
It is a male child, it is no sorrow. Female child
It is weeping, there is no. Sorrow no
Children, at that house, so. The house
Is never still, is still, is no longer. The house

/

Job came out of the house His children went in
The breath of god came along
Touched stone of the house where Job wasn't
Collapse is never complete
And each stone to each surrendered its resemblance
Face restless breathing in a pile of rubble
Words hitched up
Their skirts and minced away

/

Job enters Job pokes around He takes
The pulse of the house The ruin coughs
Dust and trips up his feet There
Are no doors The walls lie open to the sky
The sand drifts in and piles in the shallow
Corners of the frame Thickening blood on the elbow
Of a couch Through the window a tipped branch
Sorrow being held straight and upright
Job came out and glanced up at god
Like he was telling the time by the sun

Job knew not, nor was he known

The wind undressed him
And took His
Empty clothes
Took them up the street and rent them and hung them
On a fence post

/

Job's wife left him through the latched gate Her
Smell of flowered poppies stayed behind One
Self isn't enough after the sun blesses nude

/

Job left his wife through the surrounding hedge taking
With him the smell of burnt poppies flowered too early
He couldn't decide if his sin was general or

It's a real cold feeling real cold

He was only just
Hanging fire

/

Job's wife refused to shame herself She
Left no note since he was the one already out of the
House and into the parched sky

/

Sorrow ran to Job and shouted and he came Sorrow
Also came and said of all the goats and oxen and servants Fire
Out of blind heaven doors came screaming a war cry took them
  away, yes
Until all dwindled to various and subtle wastes

And only I have escaped to tell you

Job slid moaning between his mother's womb and the TV

/

Job's sorrow curled against his back while he slept
Sorrow said lover we are blessed
Job had thought sorrow was his tongue
Job thought it quiet in mouth embrace
Job thought sorrow a failed echo
Job thought sorrow was the wrong end of a telescope
Job thought sorrow coincidence of one leaf touching another
Job thought sorrow unfurling greenly along his back was his wife

/

Job thought about the portrait done by Georges de La Tour
Entitled *Job and His Wife* and the ease of possession
That title suggested
With her hand on his forehead
And his naked body turned up
Toward the light

/

A raid of ravens
A murder of crows

/

That noise is Chaldeans riding Immigrants from
The left bank of the Euphrates
Hooves asking questions of possession and use-value
If you were a felon they said to each other
And reached down lean and bloody to unwind the esophagus
Of another camel boy Who had been just sitting there watching
The revolving jaws of the camels His throat parted
Gently but with nothing to say
Blood a necklace he put on smiling

/

After god touched him so that his body canted
To the left as if under a strong wind He
Sat and listened to herds of camels dying A sound
With faulty etymology Like water whistling inside burning
    wood
He put his hands over his ears
What is the difference between
Punishment and getting sand in your eye
Job sleeps bellied under the heel of the sun
Blessed be the name

/

As it is split from the shape this blank perception
As it is split from the shadow this blank meadow
As it is spilt from the rock this water
As it is spilt from this mouth this prayer
As it is split from the body this red body

/

Satan and god like two thoughts in strife Satan
Started hanging around
What was left of the house
Hoping for a bit of attention
Or even blame from Job He wore
His snakeskin boots left over from His
Time in the garden now nocturnal
and a tight pink tank top but Job
never looked twice Always the messenger
Satan says, I know the dirt on god, he says, I know
How to keep him away from your herd
Job insufferably suffering turns his head away

In some thought or other waiting for a Sign
Roof and lintel broken like light through a prism
Splinter color blue color yellow color red like old copper
Says, Listen to that wind it's a storm coming maybe
The dust is rising from the north it sounds

Can you reach behind you and hand me those Lucifers
Job asks, finally, tapping a cigarette on his palm

/

Job headed out past the houses and fields
And the sodden mounds of livestock where
Maggots moved like white threads
Stitched in and out with precision
Into the salt flats that flipped the sun
Satan trailed behind him Do you want me
To come with you he asked
No thanks dear
Well if you change your mind
I probably won't

/

Satan fell behind looking for his Shadow
His great wings dragged the ground
In their weight too confused to approximate Flight

He wanted his mouth to be overlaid by another
His holy hand pierced through
But also figs and honey And
One kiss to justify

And then to sing hallelujah

As one body stumbles out of another

Impersonates a house

In passing

/

At dusk before the final lesson
Three silent friends sealing up their mouths
Like a mantle seam
This was after the feeding oxen
Next to Job the silent friends, silent detritus and nostril breath
Day came, they cut up their words
And offered the shreds to the wind

/

Job if you are not the truth-telling person you want to be if you are not
More than righteous you must find a place where god can be seen in
All his unknowability like the point of an orgasm or the cast of a voice down
A well where the voice winds down in a skein of sound and is given back
Changed modified in subtle ways to make it both more and less of your voice
Job have you surrounded yourself with the ciphers of evil
But perhaps grasp some obligatory hope for happiness or salvation
You will come only to grief having forgotten the only forms that love takes
And you a despot a braggart a pedophile a buggerer covetous and hollowbellied

In your greed Instead of surplus you have arrived at desolation
    The house is silent
Your wife in her private gestures has grasped her finitude and all
    her nerves
Run down to her fingers where she places them against the
    window
Waiting to see history however bedraggled bring her some small
    justices
Just enough to spread like raindrops in the dust
All her life she has been waiting for this and it has never happened

/

Let's think about this his friends said One
At a time and then all together
Fault the wires and the pliers cut Slip through to
The other side has surety but which way
Soaked film only gives us a lonely
Outline and the map's contour lacks verisimilitude
Like you lack humility
You have confused the hole in your heart for the moon Your
Morals have run thin as gruel Does god
Punish only those swimming in a ruined pool
Or does he give us a door to walk through
We're not judging you But
That doesn't mean we have to agree with your life choices

/

Prisoner of his desire
Job sits and scrapes his skin as if he
Were gravedigging for six bucks an hour
Enough time for a crisis Vultures drain swirl
Please, pick my carcass clean

And the smell of salt everywhere to preserve
Job dreamed
He was biting his own arm
He caresses his own breasts He
Couldn't remember
The last time he had been alone He
Never walked to class alone
Or worked alone or anything He
Had sat among things that claimed close kin
And when he was feeling lonely
There was always the camel boy and now He
Red pitted and upright and vacant like the moment
Before an incision floods
This was the best he'd ever felt
Or maybe the worst

/

His friends sat judicious
Three clouds running before the sun's assault
It's not that Job thought he was holy but he resented
Such an early conviction The heat banging like gavels
He must not cry Oh nevermind here come the tears
And some of the cursing that was expected of him He
Has burned up the only water in the reflection of his red weeping
skin He
Wanted a cigarette Don't keep picking at that, it will never heal
Said his youngest friend Who said I want it to heal, Job replied
But he was glad for his friend
After all who can survive without a listener

/

This could get boring
Even though it's sad

In a Rage
Job cries

They send forth their little ones like a Flock
and their children dance

The children I have somewhere
Are alive if only temporary

/

Three friends
Play dominoes in the dust
With a particular grammar
Like old men under a Mexican canopy
Debts given with judgement secure
Cough it up, say his friends
But I wasn't playing, Job says

The children women and friends even
Plump lipped boys holding orchids
Won't look at him because They
Can't stand wax eyes
He weeps into his palm
And checks his watch Nothing
Has increased only His
Vision has gotten blurry
He looks away from his friend
Never take holiness personal

/

Who doesn't want a name
Other than their own?

/

Job threw stones at the sky
Until two high-stepping angels burst
Into a cloud of white feathers and came drifting
Down onto the salt flats where their line up to god
Shorted out like an old wire Job's jaw tensed
And released in an exhalation
Maybe now someone will listen

If not there's always another way out
And he kept on throwing stones toward the rim of the world

/

In extremis all is necessary Nothing
Superfluous it is like a runner's
Body

I love you

Trying to get past the longing I heard about

All of this is about god talk

GOD TALKS

TRANS CENDENCE

There is no bridge into heaven I
Travel up and down
Out of the whirlwind
A text of terror

JUDGEMENT

Wilt thou also disannul
My judgement my

Part of the law is
The side-eye between
Forgiveness and forgetting

Bind their faces in secret

GEOTRAUMA

The ground gives rise

That is not glass That
Is water but careful it
Breaks with the same facility

Darkness is very pure
But it will no longer talk to me

This is a failure of moral seriousness

THEOPHANY

I am a servant to all good listeners

Dove rock to water oil
my prophets stand

The eye that sees them
shall see them no more
see them   again

Dwell on nothing
peace in this palm

[Silence]   stories or appeal
to God   to God

YHWH

I am only god insofar as I recognize myself to be god
Which leads to a self-consciousness in man
Which is man knowing himself in god

Send him down unwilling

WHAT IN GOD'S NAME

I wanted to see what would happen
If you behaved
Like a bit of grass
When I put my hand down to the green
Lie down
Stand up like a slow
Spring unwinding

DID THE POWER GO OUT

Strange how I feel
People not close
To me as if they
Were just a step away
And I could come up
Behind them and
With my strange breath
Whisper to the shell
Body of their ear
And their magnified
Wrist bones and
To the sweater
Slipping off their
Shoulder arousing
In me the gin of lust
Men throw levers of coins
At me and prayers

EXCUSES

I wish I had the excuse of a drunk Father
But I have only a forest of mitochondria
A cell of civilization A lot of accusations
A squeezing out of royal crimson from
The edges of shells abalone I try to hold
The delicate particular before me but Blind
Always angled toward a pressured infinity
Fetching water in the morning and breaking
Ice in the bucket The world's sleeping head
On my hips Tides on tides Skin dissolves
Into foreign relationships Clusters
Junk DNA viruses that stimulate evolution
In the center of the hidden waterfalls
Of time as my children Burn their lakes
I watch the growth of the blooming tree
Branch limping toward its final position

SELF-PORTRAIT AS JOB AS PATIENT

Job emailed his friends about his conversations with god
Listen to this, he wrote, god said
Have you ever counted the oil wells on the Mexican fields He said
And have you unspooled the wires of time on which the sun runs
And have you struck flint in a horse's nostril And have you
And then he
Receded from the whirlwind into nothingness

And then because Job thought he was talking to god
Or maybe because He
No longer believed in god Or maybe
Because he was priapic No longer sleeping at all and disheveled
And in the bricked light he killed centipedes with his fingers
And tried to give away all the money in his patent-leather
pocketbook
And ran his mouth like he was headed for an organ failure
Not even stopping for a smoke
His friends recommended that he commit himself

After all it's not the end of the world they said

Still, everyone is thinking about the end of things

/

Job sitting blinking The air around his mouth rarified
Scorched by the superposition of words
I saw the sea Job says and maybe the sand

Once did sift under such and such feet of water and rain
Dappled the paper surface and the mountains a parapet around
I have lost all skill of diving into deep water
Now no tidal ebbs
Now the rack-ribbed dogs hook meat
Like syllables from cattle flanks Dogs
And only dust on this floor Beloved
Dogs sings Job Come swaggering and
Blister this little oasis
He shivers like a child
No salve from the honey pot and hot
Pig iron hammered out like a stutter
His eyes starting from his head
And His tongue stopt
Talking like a handcuff rattling on a belt
In the back of a cruiser the officer
"How are Things Sir?"
Job closes cat eyes "Fuck You"

/

For historical reasons Job considers Fate
The machine of god and Satan
One answers and the other riddles
But riddles always keep their endings
Wrapped around them Impossible
To have one without the other
Tight as a nipple clamp
He rigged the phone so he could talk
He didn't want to talk about religion
He protests that god is pre-verbal and our words
Detached and tossed

Like a king's coin
Left spinning in a dream
That comes just before morning

/

After Job arrived in the hospital fresh and ignorant
Of the inverted language of the place He tried
To communicate first by sign language then by
Large gestures with his arms By jumping up and down By
Hooting in a deep chested voice by crying or by taking the subtle
Parts of his flesh and tearing them until the blood ran and He
Spread it in front of him like the leavings of a most beautiful coral

/

Psychologists have terrible senses of humor
Sifting in a sea of persons They miss the innuendos
That support the smaller selves
There is no such thing as a virgin past and our history
Runs like mercury like the leavings of an anthropology

/

He said, really? to the psychologists He said nothing
He said what happens in my inner house is invisible Or
Else it glows like phosphor along the seam of a rock
They gave him lithium salts to take by mouth
He sat on his cot He
Sat on the ground He put
Out his tongue and licked the floor His
Spit strung out like a bowstring

/

He found himself among a heritage of suicides
Boys in green paper balancing on the edges of chairs
Whose casual eyes looked behind their shoulders in joy
Whose feathers grew in along their backs And
Who never fell asleep Never woke
But moved in delicate circumlocution pressed down Impersonal
Question where are we heading
We must take away the phone now
Job had no one to call anyway but he didn't tell the nurse
He wanted to look in a mirror where the truth happens
Since he began burning the hills he had a great desire to
See his face like he could see the character of his friends

/

The doctor has told him
Not to kiss
The conversation with god Being
Unwarranted
So Job unclamped his mouth
From another's

Medical electricity passed
Through the hollow roots of his teeth
Left with a sort of ringing and harsh

The bell of which is how he realized
A rabbit with a Hand
On its back the Rabbit
Of Hope

Which sat insolent on a wheelchair
Right outside the Doors

Of the ward
Staring

Did you ask the taxidermist
About
Your eyes?

/

Shame was thick in Job's medial canthus
Stupid fucker he says
Shame encourages us to conform, says his therapist *because*
Of the pain
God put shame in a milk bottle
And fed it to Job
Who mewled and spat it up
The camel boys groaned

/

Job has nothing to say Job
Rubs his bare stomach against the sheets He
Wants to be simple
Folk
He wants to watch TV
And wear socks

/

Loneliness rises through him like Blood
Job jerks off into the steel sink
The faucet running with
The utopia of water

/

That's the thing says god I'm
Letting you down easy

/

Job's therapist said he needed to do work
So he wrote a letter to god ("WHO ARE YOU")
Complaining of the obscurity of Theophany
And the blindness of suffering
Like sun swallowed by snow
But why bother with just a fixed Totality
Of inner opposites God ruffled his feathers He
Was a little offended I am a god of
Victims he said

I'd rather not talk anymore Job said

/

He wrote his friends unkindly

He said
Forgers of lies   and
Physicians of little value

They wrote him back, "How a Desolate Man Ought to Commend
  Himself into the Hands of God"

/

The physician bent over the supine patient Say
Convulsive therapy will then render the mind whole Reply
Wind up the minutes and chance let whimsy in
How can a thing be true if it is not also real

Into the oxygen mask Job asleep says Wait can I
Too late says the nurse
While her fingers place the electrodes Over
His brain like a glass over a roach

Satan guilty fingers the dice in his pockets

/

Coming to
Up awake a vertiginous assent Yes
Job reaches up to grab his breasts
To make sure they are still there
[Forgetting that he didn't have any]

When they asked him Where
His pleasure was He
Could not find it He
Didn't have any pockets
So they wheeled him away
Out of the hospital
With sadness like a string behind him
Of letters Of spit Of cum Of mistakes

/

Being old and full of days

Pay up says Satan

/

Wait He
Said as the tape ran out

I didn't know
That you
Were leaving forever

/

His breathing electricity riven
Striven like sparrow to raise its red chest
Take it like a man

No

I have very little
Left

Like the charred wick of a candle
That has Burnt
Out but has no memory
Of the flame

/

Job places his hands above His
Slender hips

It is only when He
puts on makeup
For the first Time
That the panty drops

[His foreskin opened
Like a flower to sunlight]

/

[here is the deus ex machina]

No elegy for Job Job
Is still walking
No fare for the bus Because
There is no future

In transit
In transit

He has forgotten many things
He remembers
Sweet child the world is yours

Images from this time Imprinted
By light on a photosensitive plate
Show him smiling
His teeth like a geology of Finitude
Holding an ashcovered plastic cat

Here are the credences
That the wide mouth of Sorrow
Has left behind like lint
On a sweater

Job touches his body Says
I never have learned to live with a stranger

Job shoeless in a park
The sky puts on a strapless bra

In his hand
(We have seen this shape before)
Was the shape of a little poem
Was the shape of fatigue
Was the shape of another hand

Job knocked at the door of the house of Love
Don't go, they said, she'll be right down

Other homes are possible

Also the proximity of the sunlight

Unlearning the Letter

✦✦
✦

[dear c.

Occasionally I open a book

I haven't read before to thumb through it quickly. I'll stop at a page and glance at a phrase or sentence and realize that I recognize it. That I have stood before with the same book in my hand and fled through the many pages until coming to rest on the same phrase. In doing so I realize that my motions manage to outlive memory, chance, and choice. I have read too closely or not closely enough. To cross out is to add. I worry I might become unreal. And so I have stopped reading books and started writing letters, merely to live in time's pause between my voice, which is always elsewhere, and hope, which makes a little racket like a covey of quail not yet burst from the thicket. *Covey* from the Latin, *to lie down.* If you write to me as to a recently dead friend. To as many girls as men. That I might go with song, without lips. Having spoken into some other mouth. A piece of voice is not a container. A little madness is so ordinary. Listen! *To listen is an unbearable generosity. You demand this necessary loss.* Oh no we're not enemies, I protest. Put dust on the wound. Put rot in the fence. Put sun and tar on the roof. Put makeup on my face, put mud in my eyes, draw black lines on their edges, until my eyes are visible. Whether I am a man a woman an animal no longer matters, so long as the burden is off my back. Unbearable, the body. Unamended, the speech. Unlearning, the letter.

[house of 3:00 a.m.]

Who knows what the moon
Is doing. Its sensible rhythms still.
Did you ever see a body next to you.
In the dark. The soft color under shadow.
She said I thought your body.
An excellent poem she said I thought.
Without calling a spade she said I would.
Hurt your body she said I thought.
You bend at weird angles I said the.
Churned air reddish mad clenched.
With drunk subtleties. Who first thought.
Of this I said. And the world tilted.
Like I read in a novel by Hemingway.

[dear c.

Return is a tender of bearings,

using a line like a frozen stable rope to guide through the snow to an address. The strict ribs of basalt glimpsed in between breaths of road offer no ledge. The travel between us is so often violent, and I spend most of it reading to prevent the landscape from taking up too much room. Don't interrupt the car at its work. The landscape intercepts nothing, keeping its hand closed for its own sanity. The good is something missing. The good a shackle of blue syllables.

[house of blue]

The blue tune of the water.
The blue turn of the horn.
Blue benches under the preacher's
Sorrowful Corinthian brow.
The blue nails under the counter.
The blue-checkered boys and their back.
Roads and the other boys.
They never share or talk about.
I should have burned it but.
The flame never turned.

[dear c.

The child

is at the derelict grand piano in its grandparents' living room. The piano lid taped down because one of the child's siblings had earlier tried to play the piano with the tines of a fork. The child un-tapes the piano and plays it so no one can hear, the keys depressed so gently the hammer forgets to strike. It plays all the chords across the keyboard, major and minor and augmented and diminished with its fingers stretched and aching with effort. It stands on its strong legs and then kneels on the mahogany bench hunched over as though with stomach cramps. Separated by a single membrane of silence, the notes walk apart like towns. It plays all the possible thousands of chords and clusters and then plays them again, searching for one never previously heard. Now and then, while it plays, a stranger who has entered into the house by mistake stands by and talks to it. The child doesn't look at the stranger because it is listening so hard, holding up each ivory note like an apple to the sunlight. The problem is that the piano has already heard the chord and refuses to give it up. The piano has no need to be kind to everyone in the whole world. The child looks for the new chord and looks at its fingers and looks at the stranger and suffers.

[dear c.

Once a thing

is remembered, it stops being itself and starts being something else entirely. Later, when it is forgotten, it doesn't rejoin its former self, it merely ceases to exist. Memory can collapse time to such an extent that something may thus live and die almost simultaneously. There are millions of these cessations every moment, with very little mourning, which is itself a form of forgetting. Before our bodies die, we die a thousand such deaths.

[dear c.

I was there, believe me.

When you can witness your own forgetting. You tell me I called my ex from the hospital. She tells me I asked her to take me back. I fear that you remember too much. Both of us are spent. I lived weeks in a high blue room in paper clothes the color of verdigris. Out of a question comes a thing that is already taken. What use the violent needle in time's transparent vein, what use the elbow's crook if no pleasure in the blue bruising bloom. Out of a question comes a stopped mouth and a syllable. You visit my various electrical atmospheres. They crackle they coax various ardencies from my nervous system. They soften my bones. Out of a question comes a habit. Talk to me about the lightning that happened to my brain while I slept. I have no pity for myself and by pity I mean tenderness and by tenderness I mean anything that isn't cruelty like November knuckles. Out of a question come all sparrows' souls. Out of a question comes a pinhole camera. Out of a question comes a posthumous sun.

There can be no history of my body. My forgetfulness is in earnest. I check for it like for keys in a pocket. I've remained a girl all my life. Of my previous body: I wasn't there, believe me. Plant my teeth in a field and fish spring up, fish from whose tails emerge the bodies of women. Or perhaps it is beautiful women who tail off into fish, slick water dripping like sashes. A human head on a horse's neck, feathers on the limbs of a dog. Who could help but laugh at these impossibilities.

So many things for which there is no history. For instance, no history of rain. No history of risk. No history of nakedness. No history of the sleepless.

With my father's family in New York, not a single photo in the three-story house with me in it. No mouth with my name in it. I could die but I couldn't haunt this house. Less than the field mice sleek in the hay barn. An embargo on the parlor room. The dust hasn't moved in generations but still I say, I was there. Believe me.

[dear c.

A small mason jar

of violets, the violets plucked from a late snowbank and now standing on our kitchen sill. They started wilting, the small blossoms moving closer and closer to the still glass edge of the jar. Each with no face, leaning in a different direction. They started talking. I started copying out everything that was said. Mostly nonsense, nouns run together without syntax or sanity. Which becomes exhausting more than exhaustive. The specificity of object stifles narrative, since there is no particular end or movement, just accumulation. Like dust, or facts, river stones shot through with crenellated gray ridges, or anything that builds up in corners, ignored. Not that I'm complaining, you know. Exhausting, but never boring, since there is always something to add. I am no longer interested in knowledge, or in answers. Looking at the violets, I can't tell if they're any closer to the rim.

[dear c.

I was reading about synchronic principles.

Let me tell you what I got out of it: resurrection is a sense of direction.

I asked you to draw the streets of the city in my notebooks, never mind the ink blotting through the pages. I hoped the drawings would lend me their sense of direction. What is a sense of direction without a magnetized needle floating in water. I must carry the city to you and lay it on the drawing-table for you to trace. The sound of street names in my mouth like questions, like glass marbles. I never wanted to be a wanderer, I even studied to read the spoor of animals who pass on the street. The dry broken twigs. The depressed mud spurn. Who decides where the heart of the city hangs, bled pink like a purse left behind and then found by a man who wears it on his shoulder and never looks inside. The city is very much like it was last time, but this artery is nothing like a street. I plan to suffer greatly at my auctioned introduction into hope. This talent for getting lost requires effort.

[house of scars]

I imagine the slight longfingered
Marks on your body to be.
Like the scars on a whale belly.
Luminescent with time and salt.
Like coal seams or water veins.
Something to be followed.
Like silverfish. Wingless. Avoiding light.
These are the privacies.
The details that something else.
Opened on your hip chest ankle wrist.
My flower the cut my flower.
The minutes spring like your skin.
Some things you can't get clear of.
Who would want to love forever.

[dear c.

I never used to tell you anything.

This is to show that questions become an answer, given enough volume. Ask the preparator, who readies my body for the lesson. Answer a genderless and naked body, without genitals but not without sources of pleasure. In a painting by Rembrandt, my body is draped over a cold table, body opened from below like a box, observed by many eyes: artists and photographers, all clothed. My body reproduced over and over in strokes of charcoal, graphite, Conté crayon. They are drawing ecstatic loss. Hazy and faceless, the genius of my limbs undone and bruised. This is an autopsy lesson. This is an event hurrying into arrival. Under a harsh-edged light, but without vision, my sensory pool expands liquid and protecting. Without anyone touching me, long red tiger scratch marks appear on my chest. This is tender. This is an exchange. The attending figure, sleeves rolled up, holds a concealed drawing. It is an accurate study. It is most like night.

Put my body on one table. Put this letter on another. One of them will heal the other.

[dear c.

I want to tell you a story

that my grandfather told me about his time in Hong Kong during World War II. He was walking down one of the streets that ran along and behind the massive docks where the U.S. carriers were berthed. He heard the sound of shoes approaching behind him with quick steps, and then a tug on his uniform, a woman soliciting him. He didn't turn around. After that, he walked the docks without his glasses on. His vision was very poor. But even with their kimonos and his myopia, he found their nakedness unbearable.

[dear c.

People when they think about phones

at all think that the marvel is how phones close distances with a *snick*, like scissor blades meeting. But the real thing about telephones is how they un-anchor voices, walk them across sighs and hums, swell the vocal cords in ululation. Pitch stringing along behind, dropping into new laps. Voice so intimate has many crevices to fill. Your voice came bouncing into the room where I perched on the edge of the hospital bed like some carnivore much smaller than my frame. Come visit me, I said. That night I called my brother and when he answered I spoke to him in your voice, which I had recorded. *Hello?* he asked. *Who is this?*

[house of mercy]

The technology of envelopes yes.
Address a stranger is someone who.
Delivers.
An undoing. Like mercy.
Our mouths empty boots.
Lined in and out.
With imitation weather.
In all letters one finds.
Complaints about sleeplessness.
I don't want you
To
Answer this.

[dear c.

In forgetfulness

everything grows quicker, the mind skipping like a stone thrown across a lake in upstate New York, where my father drifted in a fiberglass canoe, looking for a bird as dark as a closet. I sat inside dry in cold rain while my brothers circled. Once I played saxophone on the rooftop of an apartment in Mexico, in between clotheslines and brick half-walls. Life is only approximate, but every forever is true, with its own acoustics. The light when I came over to your apartment today was the color of heavy honey held up to the sun. What comfort does, we mimic, and we hope for marvelous clouds, and burned fog, and lovers' spit.

[dear c.

When I think of Mercury

in retrograde, I imagine the pewter gray mercury of an old thermometer, its glass chiming like ice between teeth, the mercury falling down, sliding, accumulating only velocity. You break the glass and the mercury spills out into shifting puddles. With only a little agitation, the puddles adopt and then release figuration, images. You point to the floor, This is the planet of detours and delays. This, the planet of fucking, absolutely mind-blowing sex. This, the planet of boredom. The cat stalks by on thin legs. I look at the Old Farmer's Almanac. Chaos is more likely than a ceasefire, the calendar angel says. The planets are an alphabet, you say. I call an astronomer. Are you going to be such a philosophical materialist, you say. Life's as frayed as an old silver blanket to wrap the beings of fiction in. I too am made uncomfortable in the blue-black of space, which is as glossy as hair and heavy as water. You ask me, Why do you keep your stars pinned down with heavy lonely laws?

[house of TV]

Hum of tubes irrelevant. Displaying.
Its own intelligence bellied with.
Noise and static. I have a theory.
And a talent for the obvious.
In a field enormous and sleeping
Futballers pump and scud across green.
As an avocado. The colors suffer.
Conversation rudely. The warm bulb.
Gives us Tarkovsky broken like gods.
Mercy. What we forgot to see is growing in.
An old notion a new choreography.
Of visions descending from the sky.

[dear c.

Speed is older than time.

Henry Ford realized this when he launched the *Oscar II,* a private voyager to bring peace talks to the war's belligerent protagonists. He landed in Norway and I can see him there, in shirt sleeves on a cool night, recovering from influenza. He refuses coffee and whiskey and returns to his cabin. There he pens more letters to France, Germany, and Austria-Hungary in a simple American rhetoric urging peace. It seems that time had grown farther from people than he realized in his conquest of mobility, and what is left is chronically unstable.

[dear c.

Today nothing was unusual.

The chromatic density of each clock accumulating gradually. In therapy, we touched each other's hands while telling the counselor about our own lies, like limbs sticking out of wreckage. Afterwards, I thought about what it means to talk. What dogs we let slip and which we keep. What dreams we have. I don't know, do you? The color is right, but the lines are all wrong. I remembered riding in an old blue van as a teenager, in the back, head against the cold window, through an old town outside of Morelia, drowsing in the dusk. The walls colored by water, paint peeling in strips. The *tianguis* closing as the *combis* rumbled by, the dogs of memory barking at the exhaust from their pipes. The sidewalk vendors all inside, the bats gently dropping from the gray bowl over the sky toward insects flitting below. I have a passport made of flowers but no blooms left over to give to passersby, so a wasted apparition. A feeling has no outlet, so work your jaw to pop your ears as the altitude increases and the air changes all around. Can I pick a petal out of your hair? What does a gesture meant to forgive or ask for forgiveness look like? *Dime, alguien.*

[house of right hand]

Eyes on fingertips the only way
To see in the dark. The bathroom light.
Burnt out three weeks ago.
Trying to find a god to swallow.
Is like starting your mouth at your own feet
And working upwards. Fingers stutter on mascara.
Smeared like an ashtray. I want to be.
A long-eyed woman. Talk fills the night.
Like a lung. What bucket is my hand.
Carrying. A briefness drawn up complete.
From the shallow pools of your hips.
You might not be able to tell but
This is a love poem.

[dear c.

Elizabeth Bishop frequently

used the poetic technique of metanoia. It's a retraction, a reversal. Of course, a residue is left over from the words, like the outline of salt left by a receding and repeating wave. All speech is a presumption, to answer *tomorrow*. We can only say on, past the story we thought we should tell. There is no acquisition, only a step backward into something which has been hidden, like the warmth of a bed after a sleeper has departed. A spoke, a loss, no, a great loss, a restitution.

Perhaps every time I said *love*, I meant *history*, by which I might really mean *a glossary of ruptures*.

[house of Lot]

These necessary angels knocked on my door. Mercy.
Or judgement. Licked my face half-averted.
I offered up my body
To the riot outside.
The city screamed open.
And home.
Men dug a pit.
In eyes screwed currants.
Love is my first
Choice but.
Their faces blossomed.
They propped me open.
With delicate paring knives. The petal edges.
Of their faces. They shaved from my bones.
That which weighed too much.
Stoking a small fire inside me.
Between the edge of refuge.
And blowing. Sparks leaping.
Up like swallows.
Light boned and burned. I looked ahead. Waited.
For them to give me back my eyes.
I was seeing still pared clouds in the sky.
Pared clouds still.
Lighter than my bones.
Bones have nothing to do
With anything. Still.
There are the clouds.

[dear c.

The body of a wasp,

behind the head, is divided into two parts. The hindmost, the most distinctive part of the wasp, is conic, coming to a decisive point a little further forward than a thorn, while the thorax, coming after an impossibly narrow waist, is more spherical. The surface of the body is smooth and polished, with hard and individual hairs emerging from joints and legs. The hind part resembles a half-extended telescope, or armor, almost metallic, the body's segmentation accentuated by the fields of yellow and banded black. The bands look decorative. They look like shredded ribbons after a party. The wasp's singing, the hum of the love-choir. Unlike the bee, the wasp is never asked to die for another. The wasp holds no law court, is juried only by the large large sky. I believe eternally in the sting. My witnesses: a match head, extinguished on a wrist. a clock. a butterfly needle. the syrup of an apple. This is what the wasp says. The touch of the sting outstrips its pain.

[house of yes]

Fragile gladness is yours.
Crossed out. You must not speak.
To anyone for fear of shatter.
This bullet bird or shriven sparrow.
Is always telling me I.
Can't keep a thing. Turns out.
My winter bed is combustible.
Everything accommodates time.
Erasure constructed as opening.
Hold me from behind by the empty
Park pond under sycamores.

[dear c.

I say,

The better things can only be gathered with a pen.

You disagree and pick up in your mouth the stream that smooths down the stones you collect.

ACKNOWLEDGMENTS

To all I have forgotten

To Dr. Herleth, for keeping me mostly sane

To my darlings, Grae & Eric & Micaela

To my family, Sheila & Genevieve & Robin

To Jack, my beautiful boy

To Jonathan, so often my first reader, for the conversations, the drives, the music, the whiskey, the writing, and for your love

To Cass, because you first loved me, & for insisting that our life together is still unfinished

PREVIOUS PUBLICATIONS

Poems from *Letters to Forget* have previously appeared in *Denver Quarterly, Small Po[r]tions,* and *Utterance.*

A NOTE ABOUT THE AUTHOR

Kelly Caldwell was a trans poet, writer, and visual artist. She was a winner of the Norma Lowry Memorial Prize and the Cornelison English Prize from Washington University in St. Louis, an Academy of American Poets University Prize, and the 2019 Greg Grummer Prize. Her writing has appeared in *Denver Quarterly*, *Entropy*, *Fence*, *Mississippi Review*, *The Missouri Review*, *The Rumpus*, *Seneca Review*, and *Vice*. She was founding editor and co-editor-in-chief of *The Spectacle*. Caldwell died in March 2020. At the time, she was living in Columbia, Missouri, with her partner, the writer Cass Donish. She was posthumously awarded an honorary PhD in English from Washington University in St. Louis.

A NOTE ON THE TYPE

This book is set in Fournier, a font designed by Pierre-Simon Fournier *le jeune* (1712–1768). In 1764 and 1766 he published his *Manuel typographique*, a treatise on the history of French types and printing and the measurement of type by the point system. Fournier's type is considered transitional in that it drew its inspiration from the old style, yet was ingeniously innovational, providing for an elegant, legible appearance. In 1925 his type was revived by the Monotype Corporation of London.

Composed by North Market Street Graphics
Lancaster, Pennsylvania

Printed and bound by LSC Communications
Crawfordsville, Indiana

Book design by Pei Loi Koay